C000135680

A BIT OF
NONSENSE

EDWARD LEAR

summersdale

A BIT OF NONSENSE

This edition published in 2005 by Summersdale
Publishers Ltd.

Condition of Sale
This book is sold subject to the condition that it shall not,
by way of trade or otherwise, be lent, re-sold, hired out or
otherwise circulated in any form of binding or cover other
than that in which it is published and without a similar
condition including this condition being imposed on the
subsequent publisher.

Summersdale Publishers Ltd
46 West Street
Chichester
West Sussex
PO19 1RP
UK

www.summersdale.com

Colour by Rob Smith

Printed and bound in Belgium

ISBN 1 84024 457 7

Contents

Nonsense Songs

The Owl and the Pussy-Cat.

I.

The Owl and the Pussy-Cat went to sea
In a beautiful pea-green boat,
They took some honey, and plenty of money,
Wrapped up in a five-pound note.
The Owl looked up to the stars above,
And sang to a small guitar,
'O lovely Pussy! O Pussy, my love,
'What a beautiful Pussy you are,
'You are,
'You are!
'What a beautiful Pussy you are!'

II

Pussy said to the Owl, 'You elegant fowl!
'How charmingly sweet you sing!
'O let us be married! too long we have tarried
'But what shall we do for a ring?'
They sailed away for a year and a day,
To the land where the Bong-tree grows,
And there in a wood a Piggy-wig stood,
With a ring at the end of his nose,
His nose,
His nose,
With a ring at the end of his nose.

III.

'Dear Pig, are you willing to sell for one shilling
'Your ring?' Said the Piggy, 'I will.'
So they took it away, and were married next day
By the Turkey who lives on the hill.
They dinèd on mince, and slices of quince,
Which they ate with a runcible spoon;
And hand in hand, on the edge of the sand,
They danced by the light of the moon,
The moon,
The moon,
They danced by the light of the moon.

The Jumblies.

They went to sea in a Sieve, they did;
In a Sieve they went to sea:
In spite of all their friends could say,
On a winter's morn, on a stormy day,
In a Sieve they went to sea!
And when the Sieve turned round and round,
And every one cried, 'You'll all be drowned!'
They called aloud, 'Our Sieve ain't big,
'But we don't care a button! we don't care a fig!
'In a Sieve we'll go to sea!'
Far and few, far and few,
Are the lands where the Jumblies live;
Their heads are green, and their hands are blue,
And they went to sea in a Sieve.

II.

They sailed away in a Sieve, they did,
   In a Sieve they sailed so fast,
With only a beautiful pea-green veil
Tied with a riband by way of a sail,
   To a small tobacco-pipe mast;
And every one said, who saw them go,
'O won't they be soon upset, you know!
'For the sky is dark, and the voyage is long,
'And happen what may, it's extremely wrong
   'In a Sieve to sail so fast!'
   Far and few, far and few,
  Are the lands where the Jumblies live;
Their heads are green, and their hands are
  blue, And they went to sea in a Sieve.

III.

The water it soon came in, it did,
The water it soon came in;
So to keep them dry, they wrapped their feet
In a pinky paper all folded neat,
And they fastened it down with a pin.
And they passed the night in a crockery-jar,
And each of them said, 'How wise we are!
'Though the sky be dark, and the voyage be long,
'Yet we never can think we were rash or wrong,
'While round in our Sieve we spin!'
Far and few, far and few,
Are the lands where the Jumblies live;
Their heads are green, and their hands are blue,
And they went to sea in a Sieve.

IV.

And all night long they sailed away;
And when the sun went down,
They whistled and warbled a moony song
To the echoing sound of a coppery gong,
In the shade of the mountains brown.
'O Timballo! How happy we are,
'When we live in a sieve and a crockery-jar.
'And all night long in the moonlight pale,
'We sail away with a pea-green sail,
'In the shade of the mountains brown!'
Far and few, far and few,
Are the lands where the Jumblies live;
Their heads are green, and their hands are blue
And they went to sea in a Sieve.

V.

They sailed to the Western Sea, they did,
    To a land all covered with trees,
And they bought an Owl, and a useful Cart,
And a pound of Rice, and a Cranberry Tart,
    And a hive of silvery Bees.
And they bought a Pig, and some green
        Jackdaws,
And a lovely Monkey with lollipop paws,
    And forty bottles of Ring-Bo-Ree,
    And no end of Stilton Cheese.
        Far and few, far and few,
    Are the lands where the Jumblies live;
Their heads are green, and their hands are blue,
    And they went to sea in a Sieve.

VI.

And in twenty years they all came back,
In twenty years or more,
And every one said, 'How tall they've grown!
'For they've been to the Lakes, and the
Terrible Zone,
'And the hills of the Chankly Bore;'
And they drank their health, and gave them a feast
Of dumplings made of beautiful yeast;
And every one said, 'If we only live,
'We too will go to sea in a Sieve,—
'To the hills of the Chankly Bore!'
Far and few, far and few,
Are the lands where the Jumblies live;
Their heads are green, and their hands are blue,
And they went to sea in a Sieve.

The Table and the Chair.

I.

Said the Table to the Chair,
'You can hardly be aware
'How I suffer from the heat,
'And from chilblains on my feet!
'If we took a little walk,
'We might have a little talk!
'Pray let us take the air!'
Said the Table to the Chair.

II.

Said the Chair unto the Table,
'Now you *know* we are not able!
'How foolishly you talk,
'When you know we *cannot* walk!'
Said the Table with a sigh,
'It can do no harm to try;
'I've as many legs as you,
'Why can't we walk on two?'

III.

So they both went slowly down,
And walked about the town
With a cheerful bumpy sound,
As they toddled round and round.
And everybody cried,
As they hastened to their side,
'See! the Table and the Chair
'Have come out to take the air!'

IV.

But in going down an alley,
To a castle in the valley,
They completely lost their way,
And wandered all the day,
Till, to see them safely back.
They paid a Ducky-quack,
And a Beetle, and a Mouse,
Who took them to their house.

V.

Then they whispered to each other,
'O delightful little brother!
'What a lovely walk we've taken!
'Let us dine on Beans and Bacon!'
So the Ducky and the leetle
Browny-Mousy and the Beetle
Dined, and danced upon their heads
Till they toddled to their beds.

The Dong with a Luminous Nose.

When awful darkness and silence reign
Over the great Gromboolian plain,
Through the long, long wintry nights;—
When the angry breakers roar
As they beat on the rocky shore;—
When Storm-clouds brood on the
towering heights
Of the Hills of the Chankly Bore:—
Then, through the vast and gloomy dark,
There moves what seems a fiery spark,
A lonely spark with silvery rays
Piercing the coal-black night,—
A meteor strange and bright:—
Hither and thither the vision strays,
A single lurid light.

Slowly it wanders,—pauses,—creeps,—
Anon it sparkles,—flashes and leaps;
And ever as onward it gleaming goes
A light on the Bong-tree stems it throws.
And those who watch at that midnight hour
From Hall or Terrace, or lofty Tower,
Cry, as the wild light passes along,—
'The Dong!—the Dong!
'The wandering Dong through the forest goes!
'The Dong! the Dong!
'The Dong with a luminous Nose!'

Long years ago
The Dong was happy and gay,
Till he fell in love with a Jumbly Girl
Who came to those shores one day.
For the Jumblies came in a Sieve, they did,—
Landing at eve near the Zemmery Fidd
Where the Oblong Oysters grow,
And the rocks are smooth and gray.
And all the woods and the valleys rang
With the Chorus they daily and nightly sang,—
'Far and few, far and few,
Are the lands where the Jumblies live;
Their heads are green, and their hands are blue,
And they went to sea in a Sieve.'

Happily, happily passed those days!
While the cheerful Jumblies staid;
They danced in circlets all night long,
To the plaintive pipe of the lively Dong,
In moonlight, shine, or shade.
For day and night he was always there
By the side of the Jumbly Girl so fair,
With her sky-blue hands, and her sea-green hair,
Till the morning came of that hateful day
When the Jumblies sailed in their Sieve away,
And the Dong was left on the cruel shore
Gazing—gazing for evermore,—
Ever keeping his weary eyes on
That pea-green sail on the far horizon,—
Singing the Jumbly Chorus still
As he sate all day on the grassy hill,—

'Far and few, far and few,
Are the lands where the Jumblies live;
Their heads are green, and their hands are blue,
And they went to sea in a Sieve.'

But when the sun was low in the West,
The Dong arose and said,—
'What little sense I once possessed
'Has quite gone out of my head!'
And since that day he wanders still
By lake and forest, marsh and hill,
Singing—'O somewhere, in valley or plain
'Might I find my Jumbly Girl again!
'For ever I'll seek by lake and shore
'Till I find my Jumbly Girl once more!'

Playing a pipe with silvery squeaks,
Since then his Jumbly Girl he seeks,
And because by night he could not see,
He gathered the bark of the Twangum Tree
On the flowery plain that grows.
And he wove him a wondrous Nose,—
A Nose as strange as a Nose could be!
Of vast proportions and painted red,
And tied with cords to the back of his head.
—In a hollow rounded space it ended
With a luminous lamp within suspended
All fenced about
With a bandage stout
To prevent the wind from blowing it out;—
And with holes all round to send the light,
In gleaming rays on the dismal night.

And now each night, and all night long,
Over those plains still roams the Dong;
And above the wail of the Chimp and Snipe
You may hear the squeak of his plaintive pipe
While ever he seeks, but seeks in vain
To meet with his Jumbly Girl again;
Lonely and wild—all night he goes,—
The Dong with a luminous Nose!
And all who watch at the midnight hour,
From Hall or Terrace, or lofty Tower,
Cry, as they trace the Meteor bright,
Moving along through the dreary night,—
'This is the hour when forth he goes,
'The Dong with a luminous Nose!
'Yonder—over the plain he goes;
'He goes!
'He goes;
'The Dong with a luminous Nose!'

The Courtship of the Yonghy-Bonghy-Bò.

I.

On the Coast of Coromandel
Where the early pumpkins blow,
In the middle of the woods
Lived the Yonghy-Bonghy-Bò.
Two old chairs, and half a candle,—
One old jug without a handle,—
These were all his worldly goods:
In the middle of the woods,
These were all the worldly goods,
Of the Yonghy-Bonghy-Bò,
Of the Yonghy-Bonghy-Bò.

II.

Once, among the Bong-trees walking
Where the early pumpkins blow,
To a little heap of stones
Came the Yonghy-Bonghy-Bò.
There he heard a Lady talking,
To some milk-white Hens of Dorking,—
' 'Tis the Lady Jingly Jones!
'On that little heap of stones
'Sits the Lady Jingly Jones!'
Said the Yonghy-Bonghy-Bò,
Said the Yonghy-Bonghy-Bò.

III.

'Lady Jingly! Lady Jingly!
'Sitting where the pumpkins blow,
'Will you come and be my wife?'
Said the Yonghy-Bonghy-Bò.
'I am tired of living singly,—
'On this coast so wild and shingly,—
'I'm a-weary of my life;
'If you'll come and be my wife,
'Quite serene would be my life!'—
Said the Yonghy-Bonghy-Bò,
Said the Yonghy-Bonghy-Bò.

'On this Coast of Coromandel,
'Shrimps and watercresses grow,
'Prawns are plentiful and cheap,'
  Said the Yonghy-Bonghy-Bò.
'You shall have my chairs and candle,
'And my jug without a handle!—
  'Gaze upon the rolling deep
  ('Fish is plentiful and cheap);
  'As the sea, my love is deep!'
  Said the Yonghy-Bonghy-Bò,
  Said the Yonghy-Bonghy-Bò.

V.

Lady Jingly answered sadly,
And her tears began to flow,—
'Your proposal comes too late,
'Mr. Yonghy-Bonghy-Bò!
'I would be your wife most gladly!'
(Here she twirled her fingers madly)
'But in England I've a mate!
'Yes! you've asked me far too late,
'For in England I've a mate,
'Mr. Yonghy-Bonghy-Bò!
'Mr. Yonghy-Bonghy-Bò!

VI.

'Mr. Jones—(his name is Handel,—
'Handel Jones, Esquire, & Co.)
'Dorking fowls delights to send,
'Mr. Yonghy-Bonghy-Bò!
'Keep, oh! keep your chairs and candle,
'And your jug without a handle,—
'I can merely be your friend!
'—Should my Jones more Dorkings send,
'I will give you three, my friend!
'Mr. Yonghy-Bongy-Bò!
'Mr. Yonghy-Bonghy-Bò!

VII.

'Though you've such a tiny body,
'And your head so large doth grow,—
'Though your hat may blow away,
  'Mr. Yonghy-Bonghy-Bò!
'Though you're such a Hoddy Doddy—
'Yet I wish that I could modi-
'fy the words I needs must say!
'Will you please to go away?
'That is all I have to say—
  'Mr. Yongby-Bonghy-Bò!
  'Mr. Yonghy-Bonghy-Bò!'

VIII.

Down the slippery slopes of Myrtle,
Where the early pumpkins blow,
To the calm and silent sea
Fled the Yonghy-Bonghy-Bò.
There, beyond the Bay of Gurtle,
Lay a large and lively Turtle;—
'You're the Cove,' he said, 'for me;
'On your back beyond the sea,
'Turtle, you shall carry me!'
Said the Yonghy-Bonghy-Bò,
Said the Yonghy-Bonghy-Bò.

IX.

Through the silent-roaring ocean
Did the Turtle swiftly go;
Holding fast upon his shell
Rode the Yonghy-Bonghy-Bò.
With a sad primæval motion
Towards the sunset isles of Boshen
Still the Turtle bore him well.
Holding fast upon his shell,
'Lady Jingly Jones, farewell!'
Sang the Yonghy-Bonghy-Bò,
Sang the Yonghy-Bonghy-Bò.

X.

From the Coast of Coromandel,
Did that Lady never go;
On that heap of stones she mourns
For the Yonghy-Bonghy-Bò.
On that Coast of Coromandel,
In his jug without a handle,
Still she weeps, and daily moans,
On that little heap of stones
To her Dorking Hens she moans,
For the Yonghy-Bonghy-Bò,
For the Yonghy-Bonghy-Bò.

The Duck and the Kangaroo.

I.

Said the Duck to the Kangaroo,
'Good gracious! how you hop!
'Over the fields and the water too,
'As if you never would stop!
'My life is a bore in this nasty pond,
'And I long to go out in the world beyond!
'I wish I could hop like you!'
Said the Duck to the Kangaroo.

II.

'Please give me a ride on your back!'
Said the Duck to the Kangaroo.
'I would sit quite still, and say nothing but
'Quack,'
'The whole of the long day through!
'And we'd go to the Dee, and the Jelly Bo Lee,
'Over the land, and over the sea; —
'Please take me a ride! O do!'
Said the Duck to the Kangaroo.

III.

Said the Kangaroo to the Duck,
'This requires some little reflection;
'Perhaps on the whole it might bring me luck,
'And there seems but one objection,
'Which is, if you'll let me speak so bold,
'Your feet are unpleasantly wet and cold,
'And would probably give me the roo-
'Matiz!' said the Kangaroo.

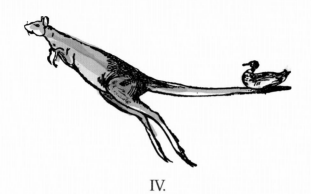

IV.

Said the Duck, 'As I sate on the rocks,
  'I have thought over that completely,
'And I bought four pairs of worsted socks
  'Which fit my web-feet neatly.
'And to keep out the cold I've bought a cloak,
'And every day a cigar I'll smoke,
  'All to follow my own dear true
  'Love of a Kangaroo!'

V.

Said the Kangaroo, 'I'm ready!
'All in the moonlight pale;
'But to balance me well, dear Duck, sit steady!
'And quite at the end of my tail!'
So away they went with a hop and a bound,
And they hopped the whole world three
times round;
And who so happy,—O who,
As the Duck and the Kangaroo?

Calico Pie.

I.

Calico Pie,
The Little Birds fly
Down to the calico tree,
Their wings were blue,
And they sang 'Tilly-loo!'
Till away they flew;—
And they never came back to me!
They never came back!
They never came back!
They never came back to me!

II.

Calico Jam,
The little Fish swam
Over the syllabub sea,
He took off his hat,
To the Sole and the Sprat,
And the Willeby-wat,—
But he never came back to me!
He never came back!
He never came back!
He never came back to me!

III.

Calico Ban,
The little Mice ran,
To be ready in time for tea,
Flippity flup,
They drank it all up,
And danced in the cup,—
But they never came back to me!
They never came back!
They never came back!
They never came back to me!

IV.

Calico Drum,
The Grasshoppers come,
The Butterfly, Beetle, and Bee,
Over the ground,
Around and round,
With a hop and a bound,—
But they never came back!
They never came back!
They never came back!
They never came back to me!

Nonsense Alphabet

Aa

A was once an Apple-pie,
Pidy
Widy
Tidy
Pidy
Nice insidy
Apple-pie.

Bb

B was once a little Bear,
　　Beary!
　　Wary!
　　Hairy!
　　Beary!
　　Taky cary!
　　Little Bear!

Cc

C was once a little Cake,
　　Caky,
　　Baky
　　Maky
　　Caky,
　　Taky Caky,
　　Little Cake.

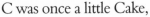

Dd

D was once a little Doll,
     Dolly,
     Molly,
     Polly,
     Nolly,
Nursy Dolly
Little Doll!

Ee

E was once a little Eel,
     Eely
     Weely
     Peely
     Eely
Twirly, Tweely,
Little Eel.

Ff

F was once a little Fish,
Fishy
Wishy
Squishy
Fishy
In a Dishy
Little Fish!

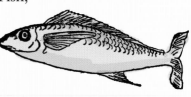

Gg

G was once a little Goose,
Goosy
Moosy
Boosey
Goosey
Waddly woosy
Little Goose!

Hh

H was once a little Hen,
Henny
Chenny
Tenny
Henny
Eggsy-any
Little Hen?

Ii

I was once a Bottle of Ink,
Inky
Dinky
Thinky
Inky,
Blacky Minky
Bottle of Ink!

Jj

J was once a Jar of Jam,
    Jammy
    Mammy
    Clammy
    Jammy
Sweety—Swammy
    Jar of Jam!

Kk

K was once a little Kite,
    Kity
    Whity
    Flighty
    Kity
Out of Sighty—
    Little Kite!

Ll

L was once a little Lark,
Larky!
Marky!
Harky!
Larky!
In the Parky,
Little Lark!

Mm

M was once a little Mouse,
Mousy
Bousey
Sousy
Mousy
In the Housy
Little Mouse!

Nn

N was once a little Needle,
Needly
Tweedly
Threedly
Needly
Wisky—wheedly
Little Needle!

Oo

O was once a little Owl,
Owly
Prowly
Howly
Owly
Browny Fowly
Little Owl!

Pp

P was once a little Pump,
　　Pumpy
　　Slumpy
　　Flumpy
　　Pumpy
Dumpy, Thumpy,
Little Pump!

Qq

Q was once a little Quail,
　　Quaily
　　Faily
　　Daily
　　Quaily
Stumpy-taily
Little Quail!

Rr

R was once a little Rose,
     Rosy
     Posy
     Nosy
     Rosy
Blows-y—grows-y
     Little Rose!

Ss

S was once a little Shrimp,
     Shrimpy
     Nimpy
     Flimpy
     Shrimpy
Jumpy—jimpy,
     Little Shrimp!

Tt

T was once a little Thrush,
Thrushy
Hushy
Bushy
Thrushy
Flitty—Flushy
Little Thrush!

Uu

U was once a little Urn,
Urny
Burny
Turny
Urny
Bubbly—burny
Little Urn.

Vv

V was once a little Vine.
Viny
Winy
Twiny
Viny
Twisty-twiny
Little Vine!

Ww

W was once a Whale,
Whaly
Scaly
Shaly
Whaly
Tumbly-taily
Mighty Whale!

Xx

X was once a great
King Xerxes,
Xerxy
Perxy
Turxy
Xerxy
Linxy I urxy
Great King Xerxes!

Yy

Y was once a little Yew,
Yewdy
Fewdy
Crudy
Yewdy
Growdy, grewdy,
Little Yew!

Zz

Z was once a piece of Zinc,
Tinky
Winky
Blinky
Tinky
Tinkly Minky,
Piece of Zinc!

Nonsense Limericks

There was an Old Man with a beard,
Who said, 'It is just as I feared!—
Two Owls and a Hen,
Four Larks and a Wren,
Have all built their nests in my beard!'

There was a Young Lady of Russia,
Who screamed so that no one could hush her;
Her screams were extreme,—
No one heard such a scream
As was screamed by that Lady of Russia.

There was an Old Person of Cromer,
Who stood on one leg to read Homer;
When he found he grew stiff,
He jumped over the cliff,
Which concluded that Person of Cromer.

There was an Old Man with a nose,
Who said, 'If you choose to suppose
That my nose is too long,
You are certainly wrong!'
That remarkable man with a nose.

There was a Young Person of Smyrna,
Whose grandmother threatened to burn her;
But she seized on the cat,
And said, 'Granny, burn that!
You incongruous old woman of Smyrna!'

There was an Old Person of Ewell,
Who chiefly subsisted on gruel;
But to make it more nice
He inserted some mice,
Which refreshed that Old Person of Ewell.

There was an Old Man in a boat,
Who said, 'I'm afloat! I'm afloat!'
When they said, 'No, you ain't!'
He was ready to faint,
That unhappy Old Man in a boat.

There was a Young Lady whose chin
Resembled the point of a pin;
So she had it made sharp,
And purchased a harp,
And played several tunes with her chin.

There was an Old Person whose habits,
Induced him to feed upon rabbits;
When he'd eaten eighteen
He turned perfectly green,
Upon which he relinquished those habits.

There was an Old Person of Spain,
Who hated all trouble and pain;
So he sat on a chair,
With his feet in the air,
That umbrageous Old Person of Spain.

There was an Old Man of Peru,
Who watched his wife making a stew;
But once by mistake,
In a stove she did bake
That unfortunate Man of Peru.

There was an Old Man on some rocks,
Who shut his wife up in a box;
When she said, 'Let me out!'
He exclaimed, 'Without doubt,
You will pass all your life in that box.'

There was an Old Man who said, 'Hush!
I perceive a young bird in this bush!'
When they said, 'Is it small?'
He replied, 'Not at all!
It is four times as big as the bush!'

There was an Old Person of Stroud,
Who was horribly jammed in a crowd;
Some she slew with a kick,
Some she scrunched with a stick,
That impulsive Old Person of Stroud.

There was a Young Lady of Firle,
Whose Hair was addicted to curl;
It curled up a Tree,
And all over the Sea,
That expansive Young Lady of Firle.

There was an Old Man on the border,
Who lived in the utmost disorder;
He danced with the Cat,
And made Tea in his Hat,
Which vexed all the folks on the border.

There was an Old Person of Dutton,
Whose head was as small as a button,
So, to make it look big,
He purchased a wig,
And rapidly rushed about Dutton.

There was an Old Lady whose folly
Induced her to sit upon holly;
Whereupon, by a thorn
Her dress being torn,
She quickly became melancholy.

There was an Old Man of the Nile,
Who sharpened his nails on a file,
Till he cut off his thumbs,
And said calmly, 'This comes
Of sharpening one's nails with a file!'

There was an Old Man that said, 'Well!
Will nobody answer this bell?
I have pulled day and night,
Till my hair has grown white,
But nobody answers this bell!'

Foss the Cat

Fop Couchant

Foß, a untin.

Fss
rampant

Fop dansant

Fish, regardant

Josh Pprpr.

Foss, Passant

www.summersdale.com